I can join i

Common Wo

This book belongs to:

Presented to

Thomas Sprogis Marsh

on the occasion of his

confirmation 30.9.04

at St Catherine's, Burbage

Children's Ministry • KKP00004

Published in (

Society for Pr

Holy Trinity C

Marylebone F

London NW1

Copyright ©

Devised and

Illustrated by

Extracts from

Church of En

© The Archb

ISBN 0-281-

10 9 8 7 6 5 4 3 2 1

Printed in Great Britain by Hobbs the Printers, Southampton

Children !
Read this...

Look !

The <u>red words</u> tell us what is happening,

the <u>thin black words</u> tell us what the priest or another minister says,

and the **thick black words** tell us what we say.

Sometimes the priest or minister chooses one prayer, and sometimes another, so look and listen carefully.

The different choices are in separate boxes...

just like this!

Adults !
Read this...

If you are using one of the official *Common Worship* books, the small black numbers in the margins of this booklet will help you to keep on track.

Please make sure that your child reads and understands the instructions above, and then guide your child through the alternative prayers, until he or she has learned to follow the cues.

The Gathering

167/1 The Greeting

The priest greets us
and we all reply
and also with you.

At Easter, he or she says
Alleluia. Christ is risen.
and we all reply
He is risen indeed. Alleluia.

168/2 Prayer of Preparation

We may all say
**Almighty God,
to whom all hearts are open,
all desires known,
and from whom no secrets are hidden:
cleanse the thoughts of our hearts
by the inspiration of your Holy Spirit,
that we may perfectly love you,
and worthily magnify your holy name;
through Christ our Lord.
Amen.**

We ask God,
who knows all our thoughts,
to come into our hearts
and make us ready to worship him.

Prayers of Penitence

We all say this prayer,
or the prayer on the next page
Almighty God, our heavenly Father,
we have sinned against you
and against our neighbour
in thought and word and deed,
through negligence, through weakness,
through our own deliberate fault.
We are truly sorry
and repent of all our sins.
For the sake of your Son Jesus Christ,
who died for us,
forgive us all that is past
and grant that we may serve you in newness
  of life
to the glory of your name.
Amen.

Which prayer
will we say?
Listen
carefully and
join in!

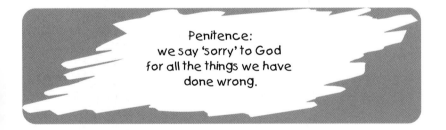

Penitence:
we say 'sorry' to God
for all the things we have
done wrong.

OR
Most merciful God,
Father of our Lord Jesus Christ,
we confess that we have sinned
in thought, word and deed.
We have not loved you with our whole heart.
We have not loved our neighbours
  as ourselves.
In your mercy
forgive what we have been,
help us to amend what we are,
and direct what we shall be;
that we may do justly,
love mercy,
and walk humbly with you, our God.
Amen.

We may sing or say the Kyrie eleison
Lord, have mercy.
Lord, have mercy.
Christ, have mercy.
Christ, have mercy.
Lord, have mercy.
Lord, have mercy.

The priest says
Almighty God,
who forgives all who truly repent,
have mercy upon you,
pardon and deliver you from all your sins,
confirm and strengthen you in all goodness,
and keep you in life eternal;
through Jesus Christ our Lord.

and we all say
Amen.

Good news!
God has forgiven
us for all we have
done wrong.

Gloria in Excelsis

We usually sing or say
**Glory to God in the highest,
and peace to his people on earth.**

**Lord God, heavenly King,
almighty God and Father,
we worship you, we give you thanks,
we praise you for your glory.**

**Lord Jesus Christ, only Son of the Father,
Lord God, Lamb of God,
you take away the sin of the world:
have mercy on us;
you are seated at the right hand of the Father:
receive our prayer.**

**For you alone are the Holy One,
you alone are the Lord,
you alone are the Most High, Jesus Christ,
with the Holy Spirit,
in the glory of God the Father.
Amen.**

The Collect

The priest invites us to pray in silence and then
says a prayer for the day called the Collect
and we all say
Amen.

The Liturgy of the Word

172/6 Bible Readings

At the end of each reading the reader may say
This is the word of the Lord.
and we all reply
Thanks be to God.

Gospel Reading

We sometimes welcome the Gospel reading
by singing
Alleluia.

The reader says
Hear the Gospel of our Lord Jesus Christ
  according to (Matthew, Mark, Luke or John).
and we all say
Glory to you, O Lord.

At the end of the reading, the reader says
This is the Gospel of the Lord.
and we all say
Praise to you, O Christ.

Sermon

We hear more about the Bible readings.

The Creed

173/7

We all say
**We believe in one God,
the Father, the Almighty,
maker of heaven and earth,
of all that is,
seen and unseen.**

**We believe in one Lord, Jesus Christ,
the only Son of God,
eternally begotten of the Father,
God from God, Light from Light,
true God from true God,
begotten, not made,
of one Being with the Father;
through him all things were made.
For us and for our salvation he came down
   from heaven,
was incarnate from the Holy Spirit and
   the Virgin Mary
and was made man.**

Turn over the page....

For our sake he was crucified under
   Pontius Pilate;
he suffered death and was buried.
On the third day he rose again
in accordance with the Scriptures;
he ascended into heaven
and is seated at the right hand of the Father.
He will come again in glory to judge the living
   and the dead,
and his kingdom will have no end.

We believe in the Holy Spirit,
the Lord, the giver of life,
who proceeds from the Father and the Son,
who with the Father and the Son is
   worshipped and glorified,
who has spoken through the prophets.

We believe in one holy catholic and
   apostolic Church.
We acknowledge one baptism for the
   forgiveness of sins.
We look for the resurrection of the dead,
and the life of the world to come.
Amen.

Prayers of Intercession

After each prayer, the reader may say
Lord, in your mercy
and we all say
hear our prayer.

> **OR**
> the reader may say
> Lord, hear us.
> and we all say
> **Lord, graciously hear us.**

The prayer sometimes ends like this
Merciful Father,
and we all say
**accept these prayers
for the sake of your Son,
our Saviour Jesus Christ.
Amen.**

Intercession prayers:
we ask God to look after
all who need his help

The Liturgy of the Sacrament

175/9 **The Peace**

The priest says
The peace of the Lord be always with you
and we all reply
and also with you.
He or she may say
Let us offer one another a sign of peace.
and we all exchange a sign of peace.

Preparation of the Table

The bread and wine are placed on the altar table.

The priest may say a prayer
to which we all reply
Amen.
or
Blessed be God for ever.

Which prayer
will we say?
Listen
carefully and
join in!

OR the priest may use this prayer
Yours, Lord, is the greatness, the power,
the glory, the splendour, and the
    majesty;
for everything in heaven and on earth
    is yours.
and we all say
**All things come from you,
and of your own do we give you.**

OR this prayer
With this bread that we bring
we shall remember Jesus.
With this wine that we bring
we shall remember Jesus.
Bread for his body,
wine for his blood,
gifts from God to his table we bring.
We shall remember Jesus.

The Eucharistic prayer might be like this, or it might be like the one on page 16.

If the priest says "We will use Prayer H", then turn over the page.

Prayers A, B, C, D, E, F, G.

176/10 The Eucharistic Prayer

The priest says
The Lord be with you
and we all reply
and also with you.

OR

The Lord is here.

His Spirit is with us.

Lift up your hearts.
We lift them to the Lord.
Let us give thanks to the Lord our God.
It is right to give thanks and praise.

We may say these words
To you be glory and praise for ever.

The priest praises God for all he has done for us
and we all say or sing
Holy, holy, holy Lord,
God of power and might,
heaven and earth are full of your glory.
Hosanna in the highest.
Blessed is he who comes in the name of
   the Lord.
Hosanna in the highest.

The priest tells the story of Jesus' Last Supper.

The Eucharist
is sometimes called
the Lord's Supper or Holy Communion

We may say
Great is the mystery of faith:
Christ has died:
Christ is risen:
Christ will come again.

Which words will we say? Listen carefully and join in!

OR

Praise to you, Lord Jesus:
Dying you destroyed our death,
rising you restored our life:
Lord Jesus, come in glory.

OR

Christ is the bread of life:
When we eat this bread and drink this cup,
we proclaim your death, Lord Jesus,
until you come in glory.

OR

Jesus Christ is Lord:
Lord, by your cross and resurrection
you have set us free.
You are the Saviour of the world.

OR

This is his story.
This is our song:
Hosanna in the highest.

OR

Amen. Lord, we believe.
then **Amen. Come, Lord Jesus.**
then **Amen. Come, Holy Spirit.**

AT THE END, WE ALL SAY

Amen.
OR
Blessing and honour and glory and power
be yours for ever and ever.
Amen.

Now go straight to the Lord's Prayer on page 18.

If we used the Eucharistic prayer on the page before this one, go straight to the Lord's Prayer on page 18.

Prayer H

176/10 The Eucharistic Prayer

The priest says
The Lord be with you
and we all reply
and also with you.

OR

The Lord is here.

His Spirit is with us.

Lift up your hearts.
We lift them to the Lord.
Let us give thanks to the Lord our God.
It is right to give thanks and praise.

It is right to praise you, Father, Lord of all creation;
in your love you made us for yourself.

When we turned away
you did not reject us,
but came to meet us in your Son.
**You embraced us as your children
and welcomed us to sit and eat with you.**

In Christ you shared our life
that we might live in him and he in us.
**He opened his arms of love upon the cross
and made for all the perfect sacrifice for sin.**

On the night he was betrayed,
at supper with his friends
he took bread, and gave you thanks;
he broke it and gave it to them, saying:
Take, eat; this is my body which is given for you;
do this in remembrance of me.
Father, we do this in remembrance of him:
his body is the bread of life.

At the end of supper, taking the cup of wine,
he gave you thanks, and said:
Drink this, all of you; this is my blood of the new covenant,
which is shed for you for the forgiveness of sins;
do this in remembrance of me.
Father, we do this in remembrance of him:
his blood is shed for all.

As we proclaim his death and celebrate his rising in glory,
send your Holy Spirit that this bread and this wine
may be to us the body and blood of your dear Son.
As we eat and drink these holy gifts
make us one in Christ, our risen Lord.

With your whole Church throughout the world
we offer you this sacrifice of praise and
lift our voice to join the eternal song of heaven:

We all say or sing
Holy, holy, holy Lord,
God of power and might,
heaven and earth are full of your glory.
Hosanna in the highest.

The Lord's Prayer

We may say the modern version on this page
or the older version on the next page.

The priest says
As our Saviour taught us, so we pray
and we all say
Our Father in heaven,
hallowed be your name,
your kingdom come,
your will be done,
on earth as in heaven.
Give us today our daily bread.
Forgive us our sins
as we forgive those who sin against us.
Lead us not into temptation
but deliver us from evil.
For the kingdom, the power,
and the glory are yours
now and for ever.
Amen.

Which version
of the
Lord's Prayer
will we say?
Listen
carefully and
join in!

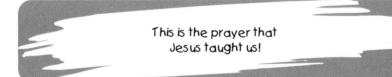

This is the prayer that
Jesus taught us!

OR

The priest says

Let us pray with confidence as our Saviour has taught us

and we all say

Our Father, who art in heaven,
hallowed be thy name;
thy kingdom come;
thy will be done;
on earth as it is in heaven.
Give us this day our daily bread.
And forgive us our trespasses,
as we forgive those who trespass against us.
And lead us not into temptation;
but deliver us from evil.
For thine is the kingdom,
the power and the glory,
for ever and ever.
Amen.

Breaking of the Bread

Which words will we say? Listen carefully and join in!

The priest breaks the bread and says
We break this bread
to share in the body of Christ.
and we all say
**Though we are many, we are one body,
because we all share in one bread.**

OR
Every time we eat this bread
and drink this cup,
**we proclaim the Lord's death
until he comes.**

As the bread is broken, we may sing or say the
Agnus Dei, like this
**Lamb of God,
you take away the sin of the world,
have mercy on us.
Lamb of God,
you take away the sin of the world,
have mercy on us.
Lamb of God,
you take away the sin
of the world,
grant us peace.**

OR like this
**Jesus, Lamb of God,
have mercy on us.
Jesus, bearer of our sins,
have mercy on us.
Jesus, redeemer of the world,
grant us peace.**

180/14 Giving of Communion

Which words will we say? Listen carefully and join in!

The priest invites us to communion saying
Draw near with faith.
Receive the body of our Lord Jesus Christ
which he gave for you,
and his blood which he shed for you.
Eat and drink
in remembrance that he died for you,
and feed on him in your hearts
by faith with thanksgiving.

OR
Jesus is the Lamb of God
who takes away the sin of the world.
Blessed are those who are called to his supper.
**Lord, I am not worthy to receive you,
but only say the word, and I shall
be healed.**

OR
God's holy gifts
for God's holy people.
**Jesus Christ is holy,
Jesus Christ is Lord,
to the glory of God the Father.**

OR at Easter
Alleluia. Christ our passover
is sacrificed for us.
**Therefore let us keep the
feast. Alleluia**

We may say this prayer

We do not presume
to come to this your table, merciful Lord,
trusting in our own righteousness,
but in your manifold and great mercies.
We are not worthy
so much as to gather up the crumbs under
your table.
But you are the
same Lord
whose nature is always
to have mercy.
Grant us therefore,
gracious Lord,
so to eat the flesh of
your dear Son
Jesus Christ
and to drink
his blood,
that our sinful bodies
may be made clean
by his body
and our souls washed
through his most
precious blood,
and that we may
evermore dwell in
him, and he in us.
Amen.

OR this one

Most merciful Lord,
your love compels us to
come in.
Our hands were unclean,
our hearts were unprepared;
we were not fit
even to eat the crumbs from
under your table.
But you, Lord, are the God of
our salvation,
and share your bread
with sinners.
So cleanse and feed us
with the precious body and
blood of your Son,
that he may live in us and we
in him;
and that we, with the whole
company of Christ,
may sit and eat in
your kingdom.
Amen.

We all go to the altar to receive communion or a blessing.

Prayer after Communion

Which prayer will we say? Listen carefully and join in!

The priest says a prayer for the day called the Post Communion, and we all say

Amen.

We may say this prayer

Almighty God,
we thank you for feeding us
with the body and blood of your Son
  Jesus Christ.
Through him we offer you our souls
and bodies
to be a living sacrifice.
Send us out
in the power of your Spirit
to live and work
to your praise and glory.
Amen.

OR this one
Father of all,
we give you thanks and praise,
that when we were still far off
you met us in your Son and brought us home.
Dying and living, he declared your love,
gave us grace, and opened the gate of glory.
May we who share Christ's body live his risen life;
we who drink his cup bring life to others;
we whom the Spirit lights give light to the world.
Keep us firm in the hope you have set before us,
so we and all your children shall be free,
and the whole earth live to praise your name;
through Christ our Lord.
Amen.

The Dismissal

The priest gives a blessing and then says
Go in peace to love and serve the Lord.
and we all say
In the name of Christ. Amen.

OR
Go in the peace of Christ.
Thanks be to God.

OR at Easter
Go in the peace of Christ. Alleluia, alleluia.
Thanks be to God. Alleluia, alleluia.

We thank God
and ask him
to send us out with
his Holy Spirit,
to be with us
in our lives
during the week.